Investigations

Heating

Patricia Whitehouse

www.raintreepublishers.co.uk

Visit our website to find out more information about **Raintree** books.

To order:
☎ Phone 44 (0) 1865 888112
▤ Send a fax to 44 (0) 1865 314091
▯ Visit the Raintree Bookshop at **www.raintreepublishers.co.uk** to browse our catalogue and order online.

First published in Great Britain by Raintree, Halley Court, Jordan Hill, Oxford OX2 8EJ, part of Harcourt Education.
Raintree is a registered trademark of Harcourt Education Ltd.

Editorial: Diyan Leake and Richard Woodham
Design: Michelle Lisseter
Picture Research: Maria Joannou
Production: Jonathan Smith

Originated by Dot Gradations Ltd
Printed and bound in Hong Kong, China by South China Printing Company

ISBN 1 844 43672 1
08 07 06 05 04
10 9 8 7 6 5 4 3 2 1

British Library Cataloguing in Publication Data
Whitehouse, Patricia
Heating. – (Investigations)
536.4
A full catalogue record for this book is available from the British Library.

Acknowledgements
The publishers would like to thank the following for permission to reproduce photographs: Corbis p. **9** (Roy Morsch); Heinemann Library pp. **4–8**, **10–17** (Robert Lifson); Oijoy Photography pp. **18–22** (Janet L. Moran).

Cover photograph of a campfire reproduced with permission of Getty Images (The Image Bank).

Every effort has been made to contact copyright holders of any material reproduced in this book. Any omissions will be rectified in subsequent printings if notice is given to the publishers.

The paper used to print this book comes from sustainable resources.

❗ CAUTION: Children should be supervised by an adult when handling food and kitchen utensils.

Contents

Some words are shown in bold, **like this.**
You can find them in the glossary on page 23.

What is heating?

Heating makes things hotter.

Some places are good for heating.

When something is heated, it
might feel different.

Can heating change wet things?

Pour some soup into a saucepan.

The soup is a **liquid.**

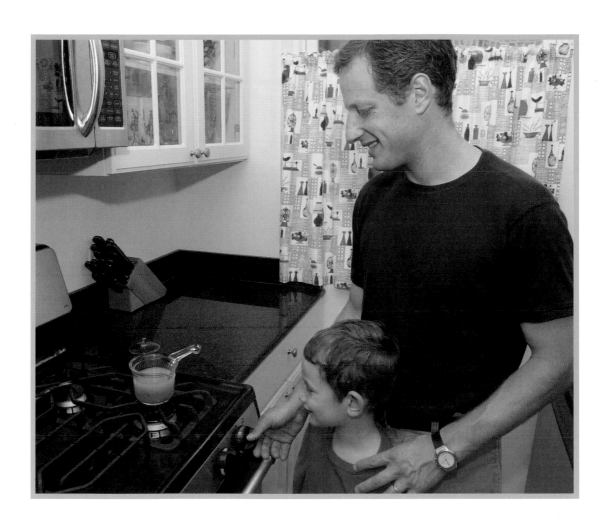

Ask an adult to turn on the cooker.

What happens to the soup?

Does heating change soup?

The saucepan and the soup get hot.

When the soup gets hot enough, it **boils.**

When you heat soup, some water in the soup rises above the pan.

The water turns into steam.

Can heating change hard things?

This hard piece of butter is in the fridge.

It is a **solid.**

Put the butter in a saucepan.

Ask an adult to turn on the cooker.

Does heating change butter?

The cooker heats the saucepan.

The butter in the saucepan gets hot, too.

Butter **melts** when it is heated.

It changes from a **solid** to a **liquid.**

Can heating change soft things?

Ask an adult to help you make cake mixture.

Pour the mixture into a cake tin.

Ask the adult to turn on the oven.

Put the cake tin in the oven.

Does heating change cake mixture?

The oven heats the cake mixture.

It starts to rise.

Then, it gets harder.

Heating the cake mixture changed it into cake.

Now it is ready to eat!

Can heating change air?

Look across a barbecue before it is hot.

What do you see?

Look across the barbecue after it gets hot.

What happens to the air?

The air above the barbecue gets hot.

It looks wavy.

The wavy air moves up and away from the barbecue.

When air gets hot, it rises.

Quiz

What will happen to a bowl of ice cream in the hot sun?

Look for the answer on page 24.

Glossary

boil
heat a liquid until it bubbles

liquid
something wet that can be poured

melt
change a solid to a liquid

solid
something that has a shape

Index

Answer to quiz on page 22

The sun heats the ice cream. The ice cream changes from a solid to a liquid.

Titles in the Investigations series include:

Hardback   1 844 43670 5

Hardback   1 844 43671 3

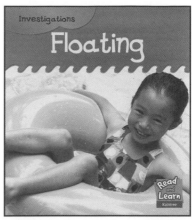

Hardback   1 844 21550 4

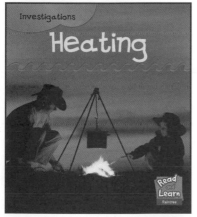

Hardback   1 844 43672 1

Hardback   1 844 43673 X

Hardback   1 844 21551 2

Hardback   1 844 21552 0

Hardback   1 844 21553 9

Hardback   1 844 21554 7

Find out about the other titles in this series on our website www.raintreepublishers.co.uk